MASSACHUSETTS

Pamela McDowell

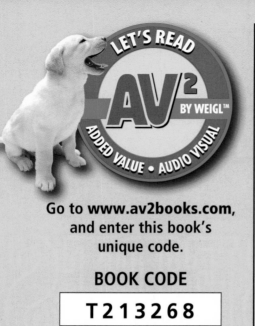

LET'S READ
AV²
BY WEIGL™
ADDED VALUE • AUDIO VISUAL

Go to **www.av2books.com**, and enter this book's unique code.

BOOK CODE

T 2 1 3 2 6 8

AV² by Weigl brings you media enhanced books that support active learning.

AV² provides enriched content that supplements and complements this book. Weigl's AV² books strive to create inspired learning and engage young minds in a total learning experience.

Your AV² Media Enhanced books come alive with...

Audio
Listen to sections of the book read aloud.

Video
Watch informative video clips.

Embedded Weblinks
Gain additional information for research.

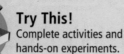

Try This!
Complete activities and hands-on experiments.

Key Words
Study vocabulary, and complete a matching word activity.

Quizzes
Test your knowledge.

Slide Show
View images and captions, and prepare a presentation.

... and much, much more!

Published by AV² by Weigl
350 5th Avenue, 59th Floor
New York, NY 10118
Website: www.av2books.com   www.weigl.com

Library of Congress Cataloging-in-Publication Data
McDowell, Pamela.
 Massachusetts / Pamela McDowell.
   p. cm. -- (Explore the U.S.A.)
 Includes bibliographical references and index.
 ISBN 978-1-61913-361-7 (hard cover : alk. paper)
 1. Massachusetts--Juvenile literature. I. Title.
 F64.3.M43 2012
 974.4--dc23
                              2012015077

Printed in the United States of America in North Mankato, Minnesota
1 2 3 4 5 6 7 8 9 16 15 14 13 12

052012
WEP040512

Project Coordinator: Karen Durrie
Art Director: Terry Paulhus

Weigl acknowledges Getty Images as the primary image supplier for this title.

MASSACHUSETTS

Contents

3

This is Massachusetts.
It is called the Bay State.
Massachusetts has
many bays.

This is the shape of Massachusetts. It is in the east part of the United States. Five states border Massachusetts.

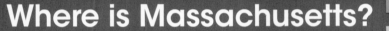

Where is Massachusetts?

Canada

N
W   E
S

Pacific
Ocean

United States

Atlantic
Ocean

Mexico

Massachusetts is next to the Atlantic Ocean.

Pilgrims came from England to Massachusetts in 1620. They came on a ship named the Mayflower.

American Indians helped the Pilgrims find food and make houses.

The mayflower is the state flower of Massachusetts. It grows on low bushes.

The Massachusetts state seal has a blue shield, a star, and an American Indian.

The American Indian holds an arrow. It is pointed down to stand for peace.

This is the state flag of Massachusetts. It has the same picture as the state seal.

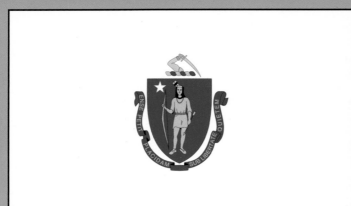

The state motto is at the bottom of the flag.

13

The right whale is a state animal of Massachusetts. The right whale is the most rare whale in the world. There are only about 350 right whales living today.

Right whales can be up to 60 feet long and weigh up to 70 tons.

This is the biggest city in Massachusetts. It is named Boston. It is the state capital.

The Freedom Trail in Boston goes through many historic places.

Cranberries grow in Massachusetts. They grow in wetlands called bogs. Cranberries can be made into juice.

About 2.4 million barrels of cranberries grow in Massachusetts each year.

Massachusetts is known for Cape Cod. People visit Cape Cod for its sandy beaches and beautiful parks. They also come to learn about American history.

MASSACHUSETTS FACTS

These pages provide detailed information that expands on the interesting facts found in the book. These pages are intended to be used by adults as a learning support to help young readers round out their knowledge of each state in the *Explore the U.S.A.* series.

Pages 4–5

Massachusetts is a New England state. These six states make up the northeastern United States. They are Massachusetts, Connecticut, Maine, New Hampshire, Rhode Island, and Vermont. The Massachusetts state nickname refers to the many bays in the area. In 1990, a government proclamation named the people of Massachusetts "Bay Staters."

Pages 6–7

On February 6, 1788, Massachusetts became the sixth state to join the United States. Massachusetts is bordered by New Hampshire and Vermont to the north, Connecticut and Rhode Island to the south, and New York to the west. Massachusetts also includes two islands—Nantucket and Martha's Vineyard—off the southeast coast of the state.

Pages 8–9

The Pilgrims were Puritans looking for a home where they could be free to follow their religion. Their voyage across the Atlantic Ocean took 66 days. Almost half of the 102 people on the *Mayflower* died during their first winter in Plymouth. The next fall, the Pilgrims invited people of the Wampanoag tribe to a great feast. This was the beginning of the Thanksgiving Day tradition.

Pages 10–11

In 1918, the mayflower was named the Massachusetts state flower. The mayflower has been endangered in the state since 1925. Its endangered status is due to human activity and environmental damage caused by logging. The American Indian on the state seal is an Algonquian. He holds an arrow pointing down to represent peace.

Pages 12–13

Massachusetts chose a new state flag in 1971. The motto under the coat of arms means "By the sword we seek peace, but peace only under liberty." The star symbolizes Massachusetts as one of the original 13 colonies that formed the United States.

Pages 14–15

Right whales grow up to 60 feet (18 meters) long and can weigh more than 70 tons (63 tonnes). Whalers gave right whales their name. The whales were friendly and swam close to shore, so whalers believed these were the "right" whales to hunt. Northern right whales were hunted almost to extinction. They are now endangered. There are only about 350 northern right whales left in the world.

Pages 16–17

Boston was settled in 1630 and now has a population of about 618,000. The Freedom Trail is a red brick trail that passes 16 historic sites over 2.5 miles (4 kilometers). The trail passes Paul Revere's house, the Bunker Hill Monument, and the U.S.S. *Constitution*, a warship that was used during the War of 1812. The ship now sits in Boston Harbor.

Pages 18–19

There are about 14,000 acres (5,700 hectares) of cranberry bogs in Massachusetts. Cranberries grow on vines. Some cranberry vines in Massachusetts are more than 100 years old. One gallon (3.7 liters) of juice contains about 4,400 cranberries. Early settlers called the fruit a "craneberry" because the blossoms look like the head of a crane.

Pages 20–21

Cape Cod is a peninsula at the easternmost point of Massachusetts. It is a well-known summer tourism destination. Cape Cod features 15 towns, several working lighthouses, and many beaches. People enjoy beachcombing, biking, fishing, whale watching, and sailing at Cape Cod.

KEY WORDS

Research has shown that as much as 65 percent of all written material published in English is made up of 300 words. These 300 words cannot be taught using pictures or learned by sounding them out. They must be recognized by sight. This book contains 59 common sight words to help young readers improve their reading fluency and comprehension. This book also teaches young readers several important content words, such as proper nouns. These words are paired with pictures to aid in learning and improve understanding.

Page	Sight Words First Appearance
4	has, is, it, many, state, the, this
7	in, next, of, part, to, where
8	a, American, and, came, find, food, from, houses, Indians, make, named, on, they
11	an, down, for, grows
12	as, at, picture, same
15	about, animal, are, be, can, feet, long, most, only, right, there, up, world
16	city, places, through
19	each, into, made, year
20	also, come, its, learn, people

Page	Content Words First Appearance
4	bays, Massachusetts
7	Atlantic Ocean, shape, United States
8	England, Mayflower, Pilgrims, ship
11	arm, arrow, bushes, flower, peace, seal, shield, star
12	bottom, flag, motto
15	tons, whale
16	Boston, capital, Freedom Trail
19	barrels, bogs, cranberries, juice, wetlands
20	beaches, Cape Cod, history, parks